ᐃᓄᐃᑦ ᓴᓇᕐᕈᑎᖏᑦ ᓴᓇᔾᔭᓯᖏᑦᓗ
ᐱᓕᕆᐊᖑᓂᖅ 1

INUIT TOOLS AND TECHNIQUES SERIES
VOLUME 1

ᐃᒡᓗᓕᓂᖅ ᖃᒧᓯᐅᕐᓂᕐᓗ

How To Build an Iglu and a Qamutiik

ᓵᓗᒨᓂ ᐊᕙ
Solomon Awa

ᐋᓐᑐᕉᕗᕋᐃᑕᑉ
Andrew Breithaupt

Note to readers: For Inuktitut-language resources, including pronunciation support for the Inuktitut terms in this book, please visit inhabitmedia.com/inuitnipingit.com.

Published by Inhabit Media Inc.
Inhabit Media Inc. (Iqaluit) P.O. Box 11125, Iqaluit, Nunavut, X0A 1H0
(Toronto) 191 Eglinton Avenue East, Suite 301, Toronto, Ontario, M4P 1K1
www.inhabitmedia.com

Written by Solomon Awa
Translated by Saa Pitsiulak and Louise Flaherty
Edited by Louise Flaherty
Photographs by B&C Alexander/Arcticphoto, Ron Wassink, and Nunavut Tourism
Illustrations by Andrew Breithaupt

This project was made possible in part by the Government of Canada.

We acknowledge the support of the Canada Council for the Arts for our publishing program.

Printed and bound in Canada.

Library and Archives Canada Cataloguing in Publication

Awa, Solomon, 1959-
Igluvigaliurniq qamusiurnirlu = How to build an iglu & a qamutiik / Solomon Awa ; [illustrated by] Andrew Breithaupt.

Title in Inuktitut romanized: Igluvigaliurniq qamusiurnirlu.
Parallel English and Inuktitut text.
ISBN 978-1-927095-31-7

1. Igloos--Design and construction--Juvenile literature. 2. Sleds--Arctic regions--Design and construction--Juvenile literature. 3. Wilderness survival--Arctic regions--Juvenile literature. I. Breithaupt, Andrew II. Title. III. Title: How to build an iglu & a qamutiik.

TH4890.A92 2013 j693'.91 C2013-901180-3

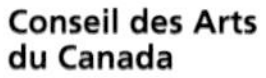

Canadian Heritage Patrimoine canadien

ᐃᓄᐃᑦ ᓴᓇᕐᕿᑎᖏᑦ ᓴᓇᔾᔪᓯᖏᑦᓗ

ᐱᓕᕆᐊᖑᓂᖅ 1

INUIT TOOLS AND TECHNIQUES SERIES

VOLUME 1

ᐃᒡᓗᓕᓂᖅ ᖃᒧᓯᐅᕐᓂᕐᓗ

How To Build an Iglu and a Qamutiik

ᓲᓗᒨᓂ ᐊᕙ
Solomon Awa

ᐋᓐᑐᕉᕗᕋᐃᑕᑉ
Andrew Breithaupt

ᖃᐅᔨᑎᑦᑎᒋᐊᕈᑎ

ᕿᑭᖅᑕᓂ ᐃᓄᐃᑦ ᑲᑐᔾᔨᖃᑎᒌᒃᑯᑦ ᕿᒥᕐᕈᐊᒐᕋᓛᓕᐅᓚᐅᖅᐳᑦ ᑖᒃᓯᒥᖓ ᖃᐅᔨᒪᔾᔪᑎᒋᔭᐅᖃᑦᑕᕐᓂᐊᕐᒪᑦ ᐃᓄᐃᑦ ᓴᓇᕐᕈᑎᖏᓐᓂᒃ ᓴᓇᔾᔪᓯᖏᓐᓂᑦᑐ ᓴᓇᔭᐅᓚᐅᖅᑐᓂᒃ ᐊᕙᓗᒥᐅᑕᕐᓂᒃ ᑭᖑᓕᓃᓂᒃ ᓄᓇᕗᒻᒥ ᒪᕐᕉᖕᓂᒃ ᐅᖃᐅᓯᓕᖕᓄᑦ ᑲᑐᔾᔨᖃᑎᒌᓄᑦ 2006ᒥ. ᑖᒃᑯᐊ ᓴᓇᔭᐅᓚᐅᕐᒪᑕ ᓴᖅᑮᓇᓱᐊᖅᑐᑎᒃ ᐊᔾᔨᐅᖏᓐᓂᖏᓐᓂᒃ ᓴᓇᑐᓂᖏᓐᓂᑦᑐ ᑲᓇᑕᐳ ᑲᓇᖕᓇᖕᒐᑕ ᐃᓄᖕᒋᑕ – ᑕᒪᒃᑭᑲᓴᒃᑐᑎᒃ ᓴᓇᔭᐅᓚᐅᖅᓯᒪᔪᑦ ᐊᕿᒍᒐᓵᓗᐃᑦ ᐊᓂᒍᖅᑐᑦ ᑭᖑᓂᑦᑎᓐᓂ ᓴᓇᕿᑎᖃᖅᑎᓐᓇᒋᑦ ᑲᐸᔾᔭᖅᑐᓂᒃ, ᐱᓕᕆᐊᕆᔭᕐᓂᖏᑦᑐᒦᑦᑐᑎᒃ ᐊᑐᐃᓐᓇᖃᑦᑎᐊᕋᑎᒡᓗ ᓵᒃᓴᓂᒃ.

ᑖᒃᑯᐊ ᑭᖑᓕᓃᑦ ᑲᔪᓯᔪᓐᓇᕋᔭᐅᙱᑦᑐᑦ ᐃᑲᔪᓚᐅᙱᑉᐸᑦ ᖃᐅᔨᒪᓂᕐᒥᓄᑦ, ᑲᔪᖏᕐᓂᖓᓄᑦᑕ, ᓲᓗᒨᓂ ᐊᕙ. ᖁᔭᓕᔪᒪᒋᕙᑭᑦᑕᐅᖅ ᐃᓐᓇᐃᑦ ᐱᖃᑕᐅᓚᐅᖅᑐᑦ ᖃᐅᔨᒪᓂᕐᒥᑎᒍᑦ ᐃᑲᔪᑦᑕᐅᑎᒋᔪᓐᓇᓚᐅᖅᑐᑦ ᑖᒃᓯᒥᖓ ᐱᓕᕆᐊᖅᑲᖅᑎᑦᑐᑕ. ᑎᑎᖅᑐᒐᖅᑎ ᐋᓐᑐᕉ ᑫᕋᐃᑕᑉ ᐱᓕᕆᑦᑎᐊᖅᑐᐊᓘᑕᐅᖅᑐᖅ ᑎᑎᖅᑐᒐᖅᑕᖕᒋᑎᒍᑦ ᑕᑯᓐᓇᕐᓗᒍᓗ ᐃᓕᓐᓂᐊᕈᑎᑦᑎᐊᕙᐅᓕᖅᑎᑦᑐᓂᐅᒃ.

- ᑑᓂ ᕈᒦᑐ

ᑐᑭᓯᑎᑦᓯᔾᔪᑦ

ᒥᑦᓯᒪᑕᓕᒻᒥ ᐱᕈᖅᓴᑦᓱᖓ ᐃᒡᓗᕕᒐᑕᐅᖅᑦᑕᓯᓚᐅᖅᓯᒪᔪᖓ ᖃᒧᑎᓂᑦᑐ ᒥᑭᔫᑦᓱᖓ,ᐊᑖᑕᒐᓗ ᐅᕙᒍᒃ. ᐊᑖᑕᒪ ᐃᓕᓐᓂᐊᖅᑎᒍᒪᓚᐅᖅᓯᒪᓪᓛᖓ ᐃᓄᐃᑦ ᐃᓕᖅᑯᓯᖏᓐᓂᒃ, ᐃᓕᓐᓂᐊᓇᐊᖅᑯᙱᖕᓛᖅᓱᖓ ᐃᓕᓐᓂᐊᕐᕕᒻᒧᑦ. ᑕᐃᒪᙵᓂᒃ ᐃᓕᖠᕕᒋᓯᓚᐅᖅᑕᖅ ᐊᒥᓱᓂᒃ ᐃᓄᐃᑦ ᓴᓇᕐᕈᑎᖏᓐᓂᒃ ᐱᔾᔪᓯᖏᓐᓂᑦᑐ- ᓴᓇᙳᐊᕐᓂᒃᑯᑦ ᓴᓇᓂᒃᑯᑦᑐ. ᐊᓈᓇᒪ ᐃᓕᓐᓂᐊᖅᑎᓚᐅᖅᓯᒪᓪᒥᔫᖓ ᖃᓄᑐᐃᓐᓇᑦᓯᐊᖅ, ᐊᑦᓛᑦ ᒥᖅᓱᕐᓂᕐᒥᒃ. ᐊᖏᕐᕋᕗᑦ ᐃᓕᓐᓂᐊᕕᒋᓚᐅᖅᑕᕋ. ᐃᒡᓗᓕᒋᐅᖅᓴᕈᓐᓇᖅᑐᑎᑦ ᐅᓪᓗᓂᒃ ᐊᒥᓲᙱᑦᑐᓂᒃ, ᑭᓯᐊᓂ ᓴᓇᑦᓯᐊᖅᓯᑕᐅᓂᐊᕐᓗᓂ ᐱᔭᕆᐅᖅᓴᕆᐊᓕᒃ ᐊᒥᓱᐊᖅᑎᐊᓗᒃ. ᐱᓗᐊᖅᑐᒥ ᐊᐳᑦ ᓴᓇᒐᓱᐊᕐᓗᒍ. ᐊᐳᑎᐅᑉ ᖃᓄᐃᑦᑑᓂᖏᑦ ᐊᔾᔨᕉᒍᓐᓇᖏᑦᑐᑦ ᓇᒥᑕᒫᖅ; ᓲᕐᓗ...ᐊᓄᕆᐅᑉ ᓇᑭᙶᕐᓂᖓ ᓴᓐᓚᕆᒻᒪᑦ ᐊᐳᑎᐅᑉ ᖃᓄᐃᓐᓂᖓᓂᒃ. ᓇᒥ ᐃᒡᓗᓕᓂᐊᕐᒪᖔᖅᐱᑦ ᖃᐅᔨᒪᑦᓯᐊᕆᐊᖅᑲᕐᒥᔭᑎᑦ- ᐊᓗᐃᖅᑲᓂᖅᑲᙱᒃᑲᓗᐊᕐᒪᖔᑦ. ᖃᐅᔨᓴᕆᐊᖅᑲᖅᑐᑎᑦ, ᐊᐳᓪᒥᒃ, ᐊᓗᐃᖅᑲᓈᕐᕕᐅᑦᑕᕈᐊᕐᕕᑦ. ᖃᐅᔨᒪᓃᑦ ᓇᒦᓪᒪᖔᖅᐱᑦ ᑖᓐᓇ ᐱᓪᒪᕆᐅᓪᒪᑦ. ᐅᑦᓗᒥᐅᓕᖅᑐᖅ ᐃᒡᓗᕕᒐᐃᑦ ᓴᓇᔭᐅᖅᑲᑦᑕᓕᖅᑐᑦ ᖁᕕᐊᓱᒍᑕᐅᑦᓱᑎᒃ ᓵᓚᖅᑲᕈᑕᐅᓚᓱᐊᖅᓱᑎᑦᑐ, ᓱᑕ ᐃᑖᓐᓂᒃᑯᑦ ᓴᓇᔭᐅᓲᑦ ᐊᑑᑎᑦᓚᕆᖕᒋᓐᓄᑦ ᐊᓐᓇᐅᒪᓴᕆᐊᖅᑲᖅᓂᖅᒧᑦ. ᐊᓐᓇᓐᓂᐊᕈᓂ ᓇᒥᑐᐃᓐᓇᖅ ᐃᓄᒃ ᖃᐅᔨᒪᑦᓯᐊᕆᐊᖅᑲᖅᑯᖅ ᓇᒥ ᐆᒪᔪᖅᓯᐅᕐᓂᐊᕐᒪᖔᕐᒥ, ᓇᒧᙵᕆᐊᖅᑲᕐᒪᖔᕐᒥ ᖃᓄᑕᐅᔭᐃᑦᓕᒍᓂ, ᐅᖅᓱᐃᕈᔾᔨᒍᓂ, ᐊᓯᐊᒍᑦ ᑑᓐᓃᑦ.

ᖃᒧᑏᑦ ᐊᔾᔨᒌᖑᙱᒻᒥᔪᑦ ᓄᓇᓕᖕᓂ. ᓲᕐᓗ ᐃᖃᓗᓐᓂ, ᒪᓃᑦᑐᐹᓗᒃ. ᐊᖏᐊᑦ ᒪᓂᖁᑦᑎᓪᓗᒍ. ᑕᒪᓐᓇ ᐱᓪᓗᒍ ᐊᔾᔨᒌᖑᙱᓚᑦ ᓴᓇᔭᐅᓂᖏᑦ ᑕᐅᑦᑐᖏᑦᓗ. ᑐᓄᓂᕈᓯᕐᒥ/ᐃᒃᐱᐊᕐᔪᒃ, ᓴᓂᖁᔭᓪᒥ, ᒥᑦᓯᒪᑕᓕᓪᒥ, ᑲᖏᖅᓱᓛᐱᓪᒥᓗᖃᐃ ᖃᒧᑏᑦ ᐊᖏᓂᖅᓴᐃᑦ. ᑕᐃᒪᐃᑦᑐᑦ ᓯᑯᒃᑰᕐᓂᖅᓴᐅᖃᑦᑕᕐᖓᑕ. ᐃᖃᓗᓐᓂ ᖃᒧᑏᑦ ᒪᓃᑦᑐᒃᑰᕈᑕᐅᓂᖅᓴᐃᑦ ᓄᓇᒃᑯᑦ, ᓴᖑᖓᓂᖅᑲᖅᓯᑎᒃ ᐊᒻᒍᐊᖓᓂᖅᑲᖅᓯᑎᓪᓗ. ᐊᒥᓐᓂᖅᓴᐅᒋᐊᖅᑲᖅᓯᑎᒃ, ᓂᕈᑭᓐᓂᖅᓴᐅᓗᑎᒃ ᐊᒻᒪᓗ ᓇᐃᓐᓂᖅᓴᐅᓪᒥᓗᑎᒃ. ᓯᓚᐅᑉ ᓇᑦᑕᐅᓐᓂᖏᑦ ᐊᑦᑖᑦ ᒪᑕᒃᑕᐅᓲᑦ ᖃᒧᓯᐅᖅᑐᓄᑦ; ᐅᑭᐅᖅᓯᐅᑏᒃ ᐊᔾᔨᒋᔾᔫᙱᑕᖏᒃ ᐅᐱᕐᖔᖅᓯᐅᑎᐅᑉ. ᓴᓇᓂᐊᕈᕕᑦ ᖃᒧᑏᓐᓂᒃ ᐱᐅᓂᖅᓴᖅ ᐃᓄᖕᓄᑦ ᐅᖃᓕᒪᒍᕕᑦ ᓄᓇᓕᒥ, ᐊᒻᒪᓗ ᓄᓇᖓ ᖃᓄᐃᑦᑕᕐᒪᖔᑦ ᐃᑉᐱᒋᒐᓱᐊᕐᓗᒍ. ᑐᑭᓯᓂᐊᖃᕕᑦ ᖃᓄᕐᓕ ᐊᖑᓇᓱᖃᑦᑕᕐᒪᖔᑦ.

ᐃᓄᐃᑦ ᐃᓚᖏᑦ ᖃᒧᓯᐅᕐᓂᐊᖃᒥᒃ ᓂᕈᐊᓲᖑᒻᒥᔪᑦ ᖃᒧᑎᒃᓴᕐᓂᒃ ᕿᔪᓐᓂᒃ- ᑕᒪᓐᓇ ᑐᕌᖓᒻᒥᔪᖅ ᐃᓄᖕᓄᑦ. ᐃᓚᖏᑦ ᕿᔪᑐᐃᓐᓇᕐᓂᒃ ᐱᐅᒃᓴᖅᑐᑦ, ᐊᒥᓲᑦᓗᑕᓕ ᐱᐅᒃᓴᕐᓂᖅᓴᐅᔪᒍᑦ ᓯᑎᓂᖅᓴᒥᒃ ᕿᔪᒻᒥᒃ. ᓯᑎᔪᑦ ᓴᙱᓂᖅᓴᐅᒻᒪᑕ ᐱᐅᑦᑐᓂᓗ ᕿᑐᓐᓂᖅᓴᐅᒻᒪᑦ. ᐊᑲᐅᓂᖅᓴᐅᓚᕿᕗᖅ ᐊᖑᓇᓱᑦᑐᓂ. ᖃᒧᑎᐅᑉ ᓴᓇᒪᓂᖓ ᓴᓇᔭᐅᓲᖅ ᓇᒦᓐᓃᑦ ᒪᓕᑦᓯᒍ. ᓈᒻᒪᑦᓯᐊᓇᐊᖃᕐᖓᑦ ᐃᖏᖁᑦᓯᐊᕐᓂᖓ ᐅᕿᓐᓂᖓᓗ, ᐊᑰᑎᒋᒻᒪᒋᒃ. ᐅᓇ ᐃᓱᒪᒋᓯᐅᒃ, ᓇᒻᒪᒍᓐᓇᖁᕕᑦ ᔫᖅᑲᑦᓯᐊᖅᓯᒪᔪᒥᒃ ᐅᖁᒪᐃᑦᑐᒥᒃ, ᐱᓱᑦᓗᑎᒃ ᐅᖓᓯᒃᑐᒧᑦ ᐃᓱᒪᒋᙱᑦᓯᐊᕐᓗᒍ ᐅᖁᒪᐃᒋᐊᖓ. ᑕᐃᓖᑦᓗᐊᖅ ᐅᖁᒪᐃᓐᓂᓕᓪᒥᒃ ᔫᖅᑲᑦᓯᐊᖅᓯᒪᙱᑦᑐᒥᒃ ᓇᒻᒪᒃᑯᕕᑦ, ᐃᑉᐱᒋᓚᖓᔭᐃᑦ ᐅᖁᒪᐃᓐᓂᖓ ᐱᓱᒋᐊᓯᑐᐊᕈᕕᑦ.

ᐅᓇ ᐅᖃᓕᒫᒐᖅ ᐃᑲᔫᑎᒃᓴᖅ ᖃᓄᖅ ᓴᓇᕆᐊᖃᕐᒪᖔᖅᐱᑦ ᑳᒃᑯᓂᖓ ᒪᕐᕉᓐᓂᒃ, ᐱᑦᓚᑏᓐᓂᒃ ᐃᓄᐃᑦ ᐃᓕᖅᑯᓯᑐᖃᖏᓐᓄᑦ. ᐃᒡᓗᕕᒐᓕᒍᓐᓇᖅᑐᖅ ᖃᒧᓯᐅᕐᓗᖓᓗ ᐊᑖᑕᒪ ᐃᓕᓐᓂᐊᖅᑎᓚᐅᖅᓯᒪᒻᒫᖓ. ᖃᐅᔨᒪᓂᖁᓗ ᐊᓯᓐᓄᑦ ᐊᐃᑦᓲᑎᒋᒋᐊᖃᕐᒥᔭᖅ, ᐱᐅᓯᕆᒐᑦᑎᒍ. ᑕᒪᒃᑯᐊ ᐳᐃᒍᖅᑕᐅᖁᙱᑕᒃᑲ. ᐃᓕᓐᓂᐊᑎᑦᓯᔾᔪᑎᒌᓐᓇᕈᑦᑎᒍ, ᐊᑯᓂᐅᓂᖅᓴᖅ ᐸᐸᑕᐅᓂᐊᖅᑐᑦ ᐃᓄᓐᓄᑦ- ᐃᓕᓐᓂᐊᑎᑦᓯᔾᔪᑎᒥᖃᑦᑕᖏᒃᑯᑦᑎᒍ, ᐊᓯᐅᓂᐊᖅᑐᑦ.

- ᓲᓗᒦᓂ ᐊᕙ

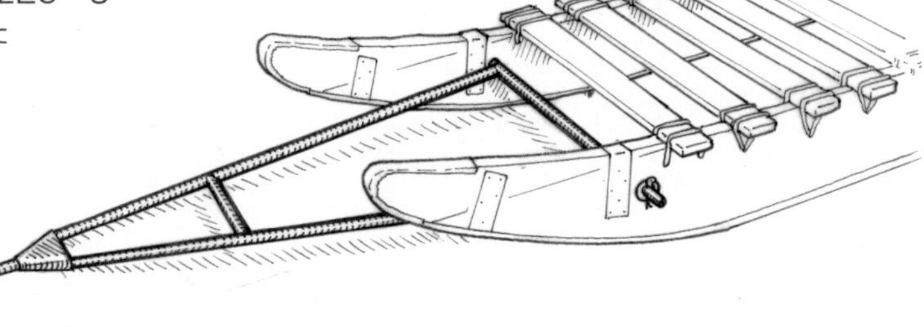

PREFACE

The Qikiqtani Inuit Association developed this booklet as a portable reference guide to complement the original Inuit Tools and Techniques poster series developed by the Nunavut Bilingual Education Society in 2006. This series was designed to capture the uniqueness and ingenuity displayed in items invented by eastern Canadian Inuit—most of which were developed years ago in harsh conditions with limited materials.

This series would not have been possible without the knowledge, motivation, and skills of Solomon Awa. We would also like to thank the Elders who participated and readily contributed their vast knowledge to this project. Illustrator Andrew Breithaupt did an amazing job with the artwork and made this series a dynamic visual learning tool.

- Tony Romito

INTRODUCTION

Growing up in Pond Inlet, I started to build *igluit* and *qamutiit* with my father at a young age. My father wanted to teach me traditional knowledge, instead of putting me into a modern school system, so I apprenticed with him in learning many traditional tools and techniques, from carving to building. My mother taught me many skills as well, including sewing. Home was my school.

You can learn to build an *iglu* in a few days, but to become really skilled, it will take a lot of practise, especially when it comes to working with snow. Snow conditions vary from location to location; for example, wind direction has a strong impact on the quality of the snow. Choosing a site on which to build the iglu is very important, too—you have to make sure there is no overhang, no snow above, and no risk of an avalanche. Generally, being aware of the geography of the area you're in is crucial. While igluit today are often built for fun and contests, they are sometimes still built for their traditional purpose of survival, and in order to survive in an area one must know where to hunt, where to go if your snowmobile breaks down or runs out of gas, and so on.

Qamutiit are very different in different communities. For instance, Iqaluit is very rough, while Arviat is flat. This has a big impact on the design and style of the qamitiit in each area. In Arctic Bay, Hall Beach, Iglulik, Pond Inlet, and perhaps Clyde River, the qamutiit are larger, because they're mostly travelling across ice. In Iqaluit, qamutiit mostly have to travel across rough land with inclines and declines, so they have to be much thinner, narrower, and shorter. There are also different kinds of qamutiit based on season; winter qamutiit will vary from spring qamutiit. It is critical when thinking about building a *qamutiik* to first look around and talk to the people in the community to see how they deal with their hunting.

Some people have preferences when it comes to wood for their qamutiik—this also depends on the community. Some people prefer plain spruce wood, while most of us prefer hardwood. It is more flexible and stronger, and as a result is better for hunting. The shape of the qamutiik depends on where you are. The shape has to be perfect in order for the qamutiik to be smooth or light, which is the goal. Take this example. You can carry a well-fitting backpack with fifty pounds in it, and walk a long distance without thinking you are carrying fifty pounds. But if you have the same amount of weight in an ill-fitting backpack, you will be aware of the weight from your first step.

This book is a guide to building these two items, both being vital elements of traditional Inuit lifestyles. I know how to make igluit and qamutiit because my father passed the knowledge along to me, and it is important for me to continue to pass the knowledge along. I don't want these things to be forgotten. If we keep teaching them, they will last longer—if we stop teaching them, they will fade away.

- Solomon Awa

ᐃᒡᓗ IGLU

© NUNAVUT TOURISM

© RON WASSINK

ᐅᖃᖅᑕᐅᔭᖄᖕᒪᑦ ᐃᒡᓗ ᑐᑭᓯᔭᐅᔪᓐᓇᖃᑦᑕᖅᑐᖅ ᖃᓪᓗᓈᓄᑦ, ᑲᓇᑕᐅᑉ ᖁᑦᑎᖕᓂᐊᓃᑦᑐᓄᑦ ᐃᓄᖕᓄᑦ ᐊᑐᖅᑕᐅᔪᑐᖃᖅ ᐅᖅᑯᐃᔾᔪᑕᐅᕙᒃᓱᓂ. ᐊᐅᓪᓛᖅᑐᓄᓪᓘᓐᓃᑦ ᐊᖑᓇᓱᒋᐊᖅᑐᓄᓪᓘᓐᓃᑦ ᐅᓐᓄᐊᖕᒋᓐᓈᖅᓂᐊᖄᖕᒪᑕᓗ ᐊᑐᖅᑕᐅᓲᖑᔪᑦ. ᒥᑭᓈᖅᑕᐅᒐᔪᒃᑐᑦ ᑭᓯᐊᓂᓚᑦᑕᐅᖅ ᐊᖏᔪᐊᓘᑎᑕᐅᔪᓐᓇᖅᒥᔪᑦ (ᖃᒡᒋᕕᓚᐊᖑᓗᑎᒃ) ᐊᔾᔨᐅᖖᒋᑦᑐᓚᓂᐊᖄᖕᒪᒥᒃ.

The iglu, or “igloo,” as it is commonly known in the South, is a traditional winter shelter built by the Inuit of Canada’s North. These shelters are generally temporary and are used for overnight hunting and travelling expeditions. Most igluit are small but could be made very large (a *qaggivik*) for special events or gatherings.

ᖃᐅᔨᒪᔭᐅᓂᖓ

ᐱᔪᓐᓇᕐᑎᐊᖅᑐᑦ ᐃᒡᓗᓕᐅᓲᖑᔪᑦ ᐊᑦᑕᕐᓇᙱᑦᑐᒥᒃ ᐅᖅᑰᑎᐊᖅᑐᒥᒡᓗ ᓂᒡᓚᓱᒃᑐᒥᐅᑕᐅᔪᓄᑦ. ᓴᓇᕐᑎᐊᖅᓯᒪᔭᕌᖓᒥᒃ ᐅᖅᑰᑎᐊᕈᓐᓇᖃᑦᑕᖅᑐᑦ ᓂᒡᓚᓱᒃᑐᒻᒪᕆᐅᒐᓗᐊᖅᑎᓪᓗᒍ.

ᐊᐳᑎᑐᐃᓐᓇᕐᒥᑦ ᐊᐅᕕᒃᓴᓕᐅᖅᑕᕈᓐᓇᙱᑦᑐᖅ. ᐊᐳᑦ ᑎᓵᖓᑦᑎᐊᕆᐊᖃᕐᒪᑦ, ᐊᔾᔨᒦᑦᑎᐊᕐᓗᓂᓗ ᑎᓯᓗᐊᖏᑦᓗᓂᓗ. ᐊᐳᑦ ᑎᓯᓗᐊᕌᖓᑦ ᐅᑦᓯᓗᐊᕋᔭᕐᒪᑦ ᓂᒡᓚᓱᖕᓂᖅᓴᐅᔭᒃᓗᓂ ᐳᔫᖅᓴᕋᐃᓐᓂᖅᓴᐅᓪᓗᓂᓗ. ᐊᖅᑭᓗᐊᕌᖓᓪᓗ ᐋᖅᑭᑦᑎᐊᕈᓐᓇᕋᓂ ᒪᙳᓯᒐᔪᖕᓂᖅᓴᐅᓪᓗᓂ ᑯᑐᒎᓂᖅᓴᐅᓪᓗᓂᓗ. ᐸᑲᔮᖓᔪᖅ ᐊᐳᑎᓕᖅᑭᒃᑖᖑᕐᒥᓪᓗᓂ (ᐊᓄᓇᒥᑦ ᑕᒫᙵᑦᓴᐃᓐᓇᖅ ᐊᐱᓂᑯ) ᐱᖑᐊᖅᔫᑉ ᓵᑎᐊᖓᓂ ᐱᐅᓂᖅᐹᖑᒐᔭᖅᑐᖅ.

ᖃᐅᔨᒪᔭᓇᐊᖃᒻᒪᓇᒃᑐᖅ ᑲᖏᖃᓇᐊᖃᑦᑐᖅ (ᕿᖓᖃᓇᐊᖃᑦᑐᖅ) ᖁᓪᓕᖃᕐᓂᐊᕈᕕᑦ ᐅᖅᑰᓴᐅᑎᖃᕐᓂᐊᕈᕕᓪᓘᓐᓃᑦ. ᐊᑦᑎᒃᑐᒃᑯᑦ ᐊᖕᒪᓂᖄᖅᔪᕆᐊᖃᖅᑐᖅ ᑲᖏᖃᕐᓗᓂᓗ (ᕿᖓᖃᕐᓗᓂᓗ) ᖁᓕᑦᓗᐊᖓᒎᙱᑦᑐᖅ. ᐅᖅᑰᓯᑎᓗᐊᓇᐊᖃᓂᓗ ᐊᐅᔭᒻᒪᑦ ᐆᓇᔪᒃᑎᑐᐃᓐᓇᖅᓗᒍ ᓈᒻᒪᒃᑐᖅ.

BACKGROUND

It takes a skilled person to make a proper iglu, one that will provide adequate warmth and safety in the Arctic climate. When constructed properly, an iglu can be extremely comfortable, even in the harshest wind and cold.

Snow blocks cannot be cut from just any snowdrift. The snow must be firm, consistent, and not too compacted. If the snow is too hard, there will not be enough air pockets within it, causing the iglu to be colder and more humid. If the snow is too soft, it will not set properly and will tend to slump, bend, and leak very easily. Crystallized snow that has been deposited all at the same time (drifting from a single wind period) on the lee side of a hill is generally the best for making blocks.

It is extremely important to have adequate air flow in an iglu, especially if you are burning a *qulliq* (a traditional oil lamp) or a modern stove or heater. Make sure that there is a little air entering at the base of the igloo and a vent near the top. It is also important not to overheat your iglu, causing it to melt—the ideal temperature in an iglu is about 1°C.

ᐊᐅᕕᒃᓴᕐᓂᖅ (ᓄᓇᒥ ᐊᐳᑎᑦᑎᐊᓇᖕᓂᕐᒥ)

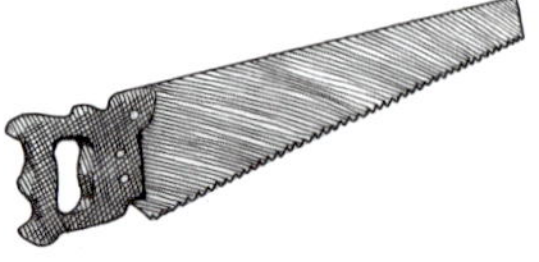

CUTTING BLOCKS (ON LAND IN HARD, DEEP DRIFTS)

1

ᐅᑎᖅᑕᕋᐅᔭᖅᑎᑲᐃᓐᓇᕐᓗᒍ ᑭᓪᓘᑏᑦ ᐊᐅᕖᑦ ᐲᑦᑎᐊᕈᓐᓇᕐᑯᓪᓗᒍ

Pass your saw through the cut lines several times to make it easier to remove the blocks.

2

ᐊᐅᕖᑦ ᐃᓄᒐᖖᒍᐊᓂᒃ ᐱᖓᓱᓂᒃ ᐃᔾᔪᓂᖅᑲᕈᓐᓇᖅᑐᖅ ᐅᓐᓄᐊᖕᒋᓐᓈᕐᓂᐊᕈᕕᑦ ᐃᔾᔪᓂᖅᓴᐅᒃᑲᓐᓂᕈᓐᓇᖅᑐᖅ ᐊᑯᓂᐅᓂᐊᕈᕕᑦ

Blocks should be three inches thick for a temporary shelter and four or five inches thick for a more permanent shelter.

3

ᓴᓂᕋᖕᒋᑦ ᐊᔪᑎᓚᐅᕐᓗᒋᒃ, ᐊᑖᒍᑦ ᑭᓪᓗᕐᒥᓗᒍ ᐲᕈᓐᓇᕐᓂᐊᕐᒪᑦ

After cutting the sides of the blocks, cut along the bottom.

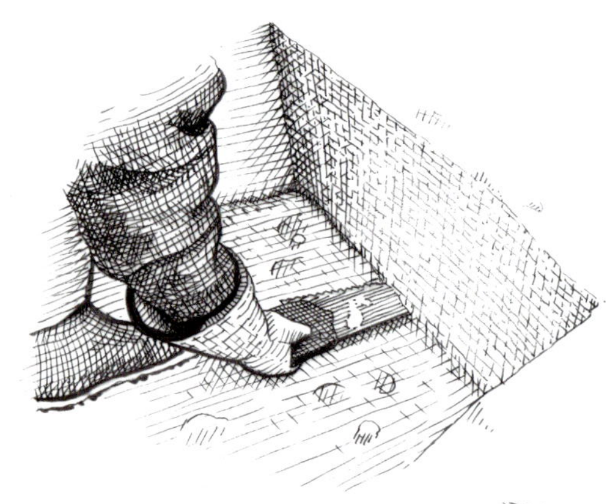

4 ᑭᓪᓘᑏᑦ ᐃᓕᓗᒍ ᐊᑯᓐᓂᖓᓄᑦ ᐊᐅᓛᑦ ᓄᓱᒡᔩᒥᓗᒍ ᑐᖕᒋᒧᑦ. ᐸᑎᒡᓗᒍ ᐊᒡᒐᖕᓄᑦ ᐲᕈᓐᓇᖅᓯᒪᔭᖅᑐᖅ ᐱᖅᑎᐊᓕᒋᐊᖅᓗᒍ

Slide your saw down the cut line and tilt the block towards you. Grab it with both hands and gently remove it.

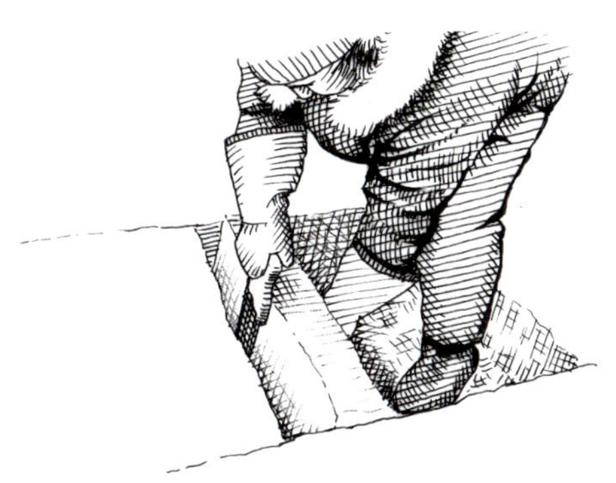

(ᓯᑯᒥᓘᓐᓃᑦ ᐊᐳᑎᑭᖅᑐᒥᒡᓘᓐᓃᖅ)
(ON SEA ICE IN HARD, SHALLOW DRIFTS)

ᐊᐳᑎᑭᓐᓂᖅᒥ ᓯᑯᒥᓘᓐᓃᑦ ᐊᐅᓚᓕᐊᕆᔭᑎᑦ ᒪᒃᐸᑑᖕᒍᔪᓐᓇᖅᑐᑦ

To build an iglu on the sea ice or in shallow snow, cut your blocks horizontally.

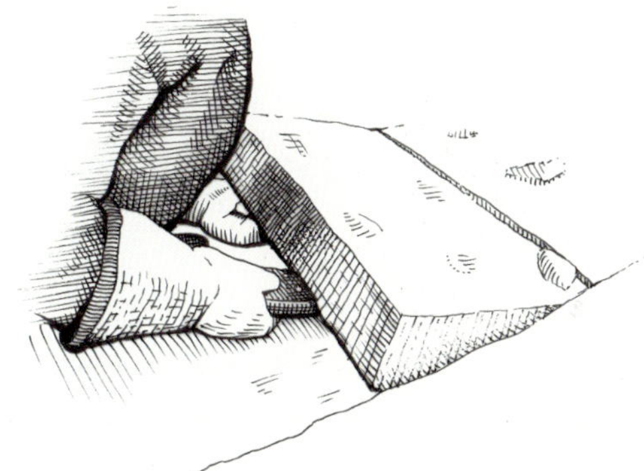

ᐅᔾᔨᕆᑦᑎᐊᕆᐊᖅᑲᖅᑐᖅ ᖁᐱᓂᖓ ᐊᔾᔨᒌᒃᑎᒋᐊᕈᓐᓇᖁᓪᓗᒍ

More care must be taken to cut along the bottom of the block to ensure a consistent thickness.

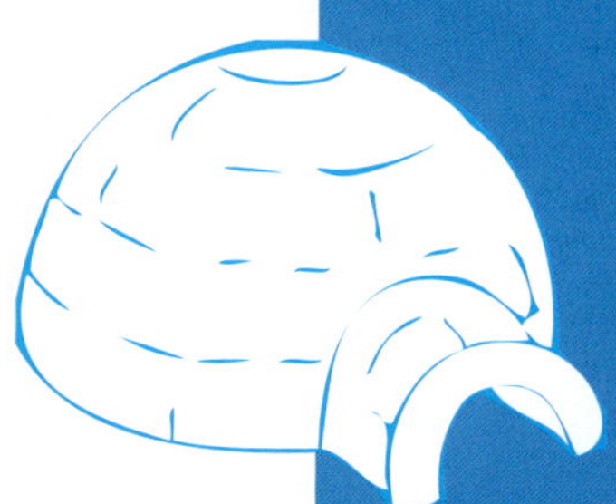

ᑐᙵᕕᒃᓴᖕᒐ
FOUNDATION PREP

ᓴᕕᖕᓄᑦ (ᐸᓇᒧᑦ), ᐃᑭᐊᖅᑎᕐᓗᒍ ᒪᓂᕋᖅ, ᖃᓴᖕᒐᓕᖅᑎᑦᓗᒍ ᖄᖕᒐ ᑕᒪᓐᓇ ᐊᐅᕕᖅᐱᑦ ᑐᙵᕕᒋᓂᐊᖅᑕᖕᒐ.

With your snow knife, using a horizontal chopping stroke, loosen the top inch of snow where your first row of blocks will rest.

ᐊᕆᓗᐊ
FIRST ROW

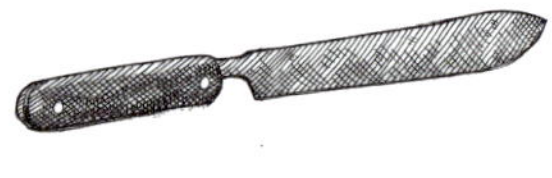

ᐊᐅᕕᖅ ᓯᕗᓪᓕᖅᐹᖅ ᐃᓚᙵᖅᓗᒍ ᒪᓂᖅᑲᒥᑦ ᖁᒻᒧᖕᒐᔮᓕᖅᑎᑦᓗᒍ

Taper the first row of blocks gently from the surface of the snow to create the spiral shape of the iglu.

ᐊᐅᕕᒃᓯᕐᓂᖅ ᐃᓗᓪᓛᓪᓚᓂᑦ
INTERIOR BLOCKS

ᐊᐅᕕᒃᓯᕐᕕᒋᖅᑲᐅᓯᕐᓂᑦ
ᑲᔪᓯᑐᐃᓐᓇᕐᓗᒍ ᐃᓗᐊᓂᑦ
ᐊᕙᓗᔾᔪᑎᒐᔭᖅᖢᓂ ᐃᒡᓗᕕᒐᕐᒧᑦ

Continue cutting blocks from the inside of the iglu to build the walls.

ᐋᖅᑭᑦᑎᐊᕆᐊᖅᑲᕐᓂᖓ ᖃᓪᓕᐅᑎᓂᐊᖅᑐᒧᑦ
SURFACE PREP

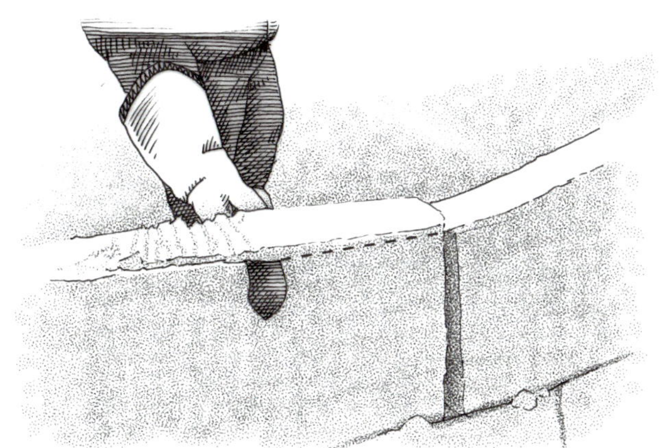

ᒪᓂᖅᑲᒡᔮᒥᓗᒍ ᖄᖓ ᖃᓪᓕᑎᖅᑲᕈᓐᓇᕐᑯᑦᑐᒍ

Smooth off the top edges of the blocks in preparation for the next layer.

ᐊᐅᕖᑦ ᐃᓕᐅᖅᑲᕐᓂᖕᒋᑦ
SETTING BLOCKS

ᐃᓂᖅᑎᑦᑎᓂᖅ ᐊᐅᕕᕐᓂᒃ ᐅᔾᔨᕆᑦᑎᐊᕆᐊᖅᑲᒪᕆᒃᑐᖅ ᐃᒡᓗᓕᐅᕐᓗᓂ. ᓇᓗᓇᐃᖅᓯᒪᔪᑦ ᐊᑖᓂ ᐱᔭᕆᐊᖅᑲᕐᓂᖕᒋᑦ

Setting the blocks is the most important part of building the iglu. Follow the steps below to properly set your blocks.

1 ᐊᐅᕕᖅ ᐃᓕᓗᒍ ᓯᕗᓪᓕᐅᖅᑲᐅᔪᒧᑦ ᐊᐳᖅᑎᓪᓗᒍ

Place the new block on the wall and slide it up to the last block you set.

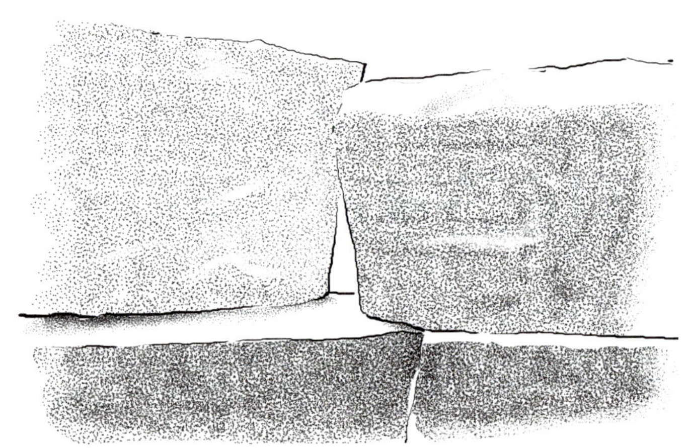

2 ᐃᓚᓐᖖᒐᖅᑐᒍ ᐊᒃᑐᐊᓗᐊᖅᓂᖕᒐᒍᑦ
ᑲᑎᑦᑎᐊᕈᓐᓇᖅᑯᓪᓗᒍ ᐃᒻᒥᖕᓄᑦ

Cut the connecting edge of the new block to fit the contour of the last block.

3 ᐃᓚᓐᖖᒐᖅᐸᓪᓚᐊᓗᒍ
ᓈᒻᒪᒃᓯᓇᓱᐊᖅᓂᖕᒐᓂ
ᐋᖅᑭᑦᑎᐊᕈᓐᓇᖅᑯᓪᓗᒍ

Continue to slice your knife down the connecting edge, while pushing the new block into the last one.

4 ᓴᕕᖕᒧᑦ (ᐸᓇᒧᑦ) ᐊᑖ ᒪᓂᖅᑲᒃᓴᖅᓗᒍ
ᐃᓚᕐᑎᐊᖅᓯᒪᔪᓐᓇᖅᑯᑦᓗᒍ

Use your knife to slice along the bottom of the new block to create a solid joint.

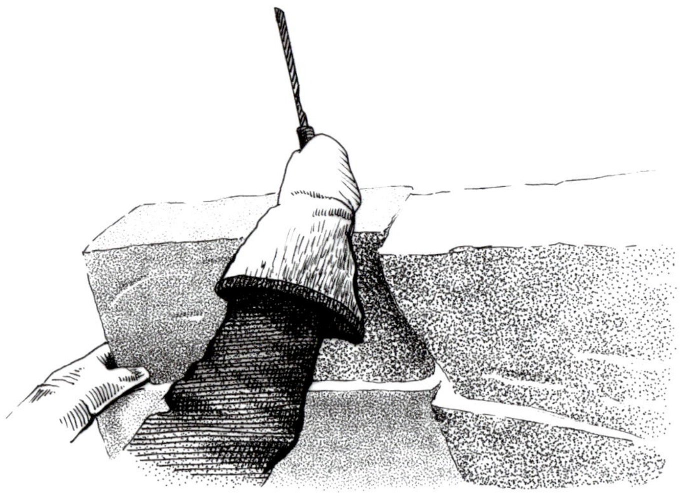

5 ᐊᐅᕕᖅᐱᑦ ᑕᓚᖅᐱᖕᒑᖕᒐᒍᑦ ᐊᒡᒐᖕᓄᑦ ᑲᓯᒡᓗᒍ
ᐊᕐᑕᑕᕈᓐᓇᖅᑯᑦᓗᒍ

Firmly tap down the right side of the block with your hand to position it tightly in the wall.

ᐅᒃᑯᐊᓕᐅᕐᓂᖅ
CUTTING DOOR

ᐅᒃᑯᐊᓕᐅᕈᓐᓇᖅᑐᖅ
ᐱᐊᓂᓪᓚᓇᖕᒋᒃᑲᓗᐊᖅᑎᓪᓗᒍ
ᐃᓱᐅᖅᑲᐃᔭᓇᐊᕐᑲᕐᓂᐊᕋᕕᑦ ᐊᐅᕕᕐᓂᒃ
ᐱᐊᓂᒍᓐᓇᕐᑯᓪᓗᒍ ᐃᒡᓗᓕᐊᓇᔭᐃᑦ

Once three quarters of the iglu is complete, cut the doorway. You may need to bring blocks in through the door to complete the iglu.

ᐊᐅᕕᖅ ᑭᖑᓪᓕᖅᐹᖅ
FINAL BLOCK

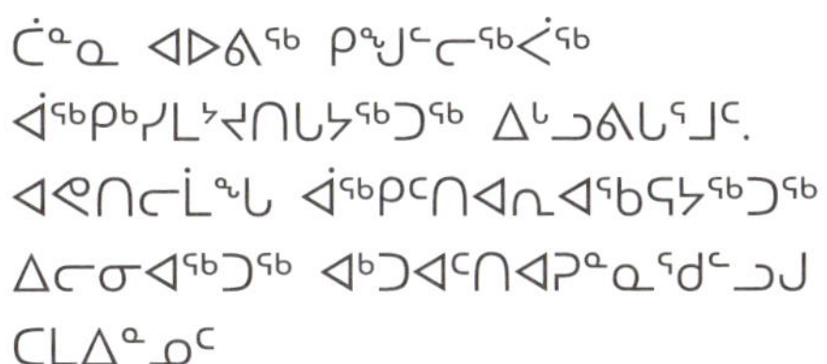

ᑖᓇ ᐊᐅᕕᖅ ᑭᖑᓪᓕᖅᐹᖅ
ᐋᖅᑭᒃᓯᒪᔾᔪᑎᒐᔭᖅᑐᖅ ᐃᒡᓗᕕᒐᕐᒧᑦ.
ᐊᕙᑎᓕᒫᖕᒐ ᐋᖅᑭᑦᑎᐊᓇᐊᕐᑲᕋᔭᖅᑐᖅ
ᐃᓕᓂᐊᖅᑐᖅ ᐊᒃᑐᐊᑦᑎᐊᕈᓐᓇᕐᑯᓪᓗᒍ
ᑕᒪᐃᓐᓄᑦ

The final block is set in place like a keystone. It is shaped so that it makes contact with the edges of each of the other blocks.

ᐃᒡᓗ IGLU

ᐅᑦᓯᒃᓴᐃᓂᖅ
FILLING GAPS

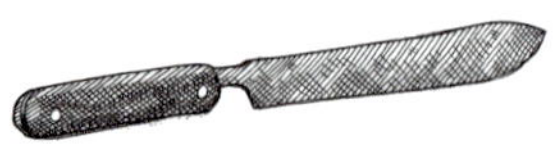

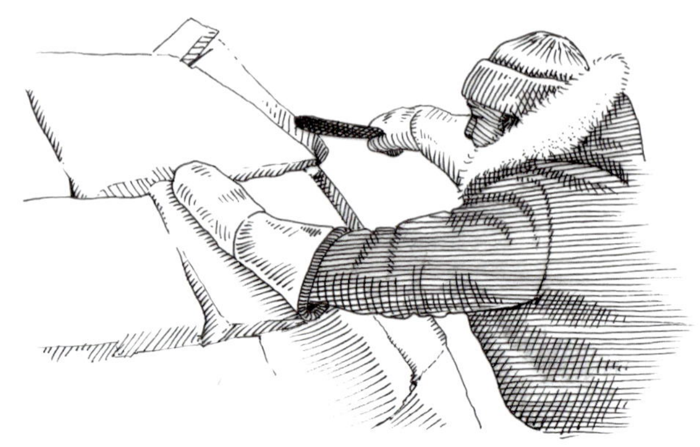

ᐃᓛᓐᓂᒃᑯᑦ ᐊᐅᕕᑦ ᐊᑯᓐᓂᖏᑎᒍᑦ ᐊᖕᒪᓂᖅᑲᓲᖕᒍᖕᒪᑦ. ᐅᑦᓯᒃᓴᐃᓂᐊᖅᑐᓂ ᐃᒪᓐᓇ ᐱᔭᓇᐊᓛᑦ

There are likely to be some gaps between a few of your blocks. These gaps are sometimes too large. If that is the case, use the following technique to fill them.

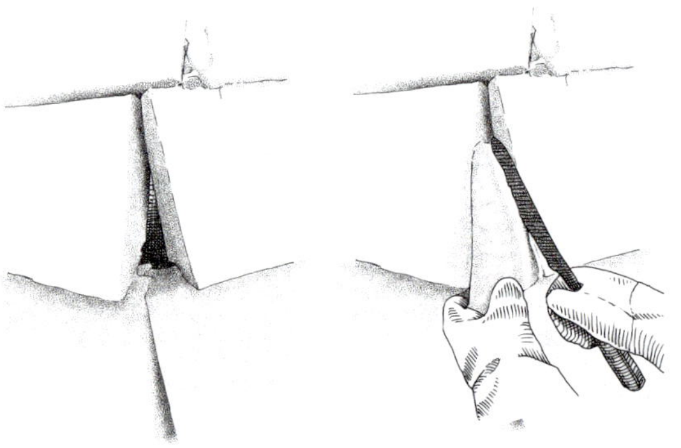

1 ᐅᑦᓯᓇᕐᔪᑎᒋᓂᐊᖅᑕᐃᑦ ᐊᖏᓂᖅᓴᐅᑖᖅᔪᓪᓗᒍ ᐊᖕᒪᔪᐊᓂᑦ. ᐸᑎᒻᒥᓗᒍ ᑭᒡᓚᐊᒍᑦᓗ ᐃᓚᖖᒐᖅᐸᑦᓚᐊᓗᒍ ᐃᓗᒻᒧᑦ ᓇᖅᑭᑉᐸᑦᓚᐊᓗᒍᓗ.

Cut a piece of snow a little larger than the gap. Hold it in place and slowly trim the edges while pushing it into the gap.

2 ᐃᓗᒻᒧᑦ ᐋᖅᑭᒃᐸᑦᓚᐊᔪᓐᓇᖅᒪᑦ ᐅᑦᓯᓇᕐᔪᑎᒋᔭᐃᑦ.

The piece will work its way into the gap and seal it off.

ᐃᓗᐊᑕ ᓴᓂᕌ
INTERIOR WALLS

ᐊᐅᕕᖅ ᐃᓗᓐᒍᓐᒐᔮᕈᓂ ᑯᑐᑰᓂᖅᓴᐅᒐᔭᖅᑐᖅ ᐃᓗᒻᒧᑦ ᐅᖅᑰᓯᒃᐸᑦ ᐃᒡᓗᕕᒐᖅ

A block that overlaps the row below it will produce water droplets when the iglu warms up, which will fall onto people below.

ᐃᓗᑦᑐᐅᓗᐊᖅᑕᐃᑐᒪᒋᐊᖅᑲᖅᑐᑦ ᑯᑐᑰᑯᓇᒍ ᐃᓗᒻᒧᑦ

Ensuring the blocks are inset from the row below it will allow any water droplets to run down the walls of the iglu to the floor.

ᖃᐅᔨᒪᔭᕆᐊᓖᑦ ᐱᔪᓐᓇᕈᑕᐅᕙᒃᑐᑦ ᑐ
TIPS AND TRICKS

ᐊᐅᕕᒃᓴᕐᓂᖅ:
ᐊᐅᕕᒃᓴᕐᓗᓂ ᐃᖅᑲᐅᒪᕆᐊᖃᖅᑐᖅ ᐃᓗᒻᒧᑦ ᖁᕐᖁᙱᔮᕆᐊᖃᖅᑐᖅ. ᖁᕐᖁᙱᔮᑦᑎᐊᙵᕆᑐᐊᕈᓂ ᐊᐅᕕᖅ ᐲᕐᓭᐅᑎᕆᔪᓐᓇᕐᔭᙱᑦᑐᖅ ᐃᓂᕆᔭᙱᓂᑦ.

ᑐᙵᕕᐅᓃᑦᑐᖅ ᐊᐅᕖᑦ:
ᑐᙵᕕᐊᓃᑦᑐᖅ ᒪᓂᖅᑲᒧᑦ ᐊᒃᑐᐊᔪᑦ ᐃᓗᒻᒧᑦ ᐅᕕᙱᓈᕆᐊᖃᖅᑐᑦ. ᑕᐃᒪᐃᑦᑎᙱᒃᐸᑕ ᑭᖑᓂᖏᑦ ᑕᒪᒃᑯᐊ ᒪᑦᑕᒃᓴᕐᓂᐅᓴᑐᐃᓐᓇᕐᒪᑕ ᐃᒻᒥᖕᓄᑦ.

ᐊᓂᖅᓵᑑᑎᒃᓴᖓ ᑲᖏᐊ (ᕿᖓᖓ):
ᐃᒡᓗᕕᒐᖅ ᑲᖏᖅᑲᑦᑎᐊᓇᐊᖅᑲᖅᑐᖅ (ᕿᖓᖅᑲᑦᑎᐊᓇᐊᖅᑲᖅᑐᖅ) ᐊᖓᔪᐊᕐᔪᖅᑲᕐᓗᓂ ᐊᑖᒍᑦ ᐊᒻᒪᓗᑦᑕᐅᖅ ᑲᖏᑦᑎᖅᓯᒪᓗᓂ ᖁᑦᑎᖅᐸᓯᐊᒍᑦ. ᐱᔭᓇᐊᖅᒪᓇᒃᑐᖅ ᐅᖅᑰᓴᐅᑎᖅᑲᕐᓂᐊᑐᐊᕐᓗᓂ ᖁᓪᓕᕐᒥᒃ ᓱᐴᔫᕐᒥᒡᓘᓐᓃᑦ.

ᓇᓐᓂᓇᔭᖓ ᐃᒡᓗᕕᒐᐅᑉ:
ᐅᕕᙱᔭᖅᑐᒥ ᐃᒡᓗᓕᐅᕐᓂᐊᕈᕕᑦ ᐊᑎᖕᓂᖕᒐᔫᖅᑳᓇᐊᖅᑲᖅᑐᖅ. ᐅᒃᑯᐊᓕᐅᕐᓗᒍᓗ ᐊᖑᓇᐅᑉ ᐅᖅᑯᓇᖕᒫᖅᑕᖕᒐᓂᑦ.

Cutting Blocks:
When cutting blocks, remember that they should be slightly wider at the top than at the bottom. If you do not angle your saw to allow for this, you will not be able to remove the block from the snow.

First Row:
When spiralling the first row of blocks from the ground slowly upward, remember to also tilt them slightly inward. Following this angle with subsequent blocks will naturally create a dome shape for the iglu.

Ventilation:
Make sure that your iglu is properly ventilated by making sure there is a vent at the bottom of your iglu and a vent near the top. This is extremely important if you plan on lighting a qulliq or a stove.

Iglu Placement:
If you are building your iglu on a slight slope, make sure that the full height of the first spiralling row is on the downward side. Place your doorway facing away from the windward side.

ᖃᒧᑏᒃ QAMUTIIK

© RON WASSINK

© RON WASSINK

ᐅᑭᐅᖅᑕᖅᑐᒥᐅᓄᑦ **ᖃᒧᑏᑦ** ᐊᑐᖅᑕᐅᔭᓇᐊᖅᑲᒻᒪᓇᒃᓯᒪᕗᑦ. ᐊᑦᑕᕐᓇᖕᒋᒃᓱᑎᒃ, ᐊᔾᔨᐅᖕᒋᓐᒪᓇᒃᓱᑎᒃ ᐱᔪᓐᓇᐅᑎᓪᒪᓇᐅᑦᑐᑎᑦᑐ ᑕᐃᒪᙵᓂᑦ.

The **qamutiik** is an essential tool in the far north. Its versatility, unique construction, and dependability have allowed it to endure over time.

ᖃᐅᔨᒪᔭᐅᓂᖓ

ᖃᒧᔨᐅᖃᑦᑕᓚᐅᖅᓯᒪᕗᑦ ᓴᐅᓂᕕᓂᕐᓂᑦ, ᑎᔾᔭᕐᓗᑯᕕᓂᕐᓂᒡᓗ ᕿᔪᖕᓂᒃ, ᓇᒡᔪᕕᓂᕐᓂᒃ, ᐊᒃᓱᓈᒥᑦᓗ ᓇᑦᑎᕋᔭᖕᓂᒃ. ᖃᒧᔨᐅᖅᐸᓚᐅᖅᐳᑦ ᐃᖃᓗᕕᓂᕐᓂᒃ ᖁᐊᓂᒃ ᐸᑎᒃᓯᑎᓯᒪᔭᐅᓪᓗᑎᒃ ᐊᒥᕐᓄᑦ ᑲᐅᖕᓄᓪᓘᓐᓃᑦ. ᐱᐊᒃᓴᐅᑎᖅᑲᖅᐸᓚᐅᖅᐳᑦ ᐃᔾᔪᖅᓯᒪᓪᓗᒍ ᓯᕐᒥᖅᓯᒪᓪᓗᒍᓗ, ᐊᕐᕕᐅᓪᓘᓐᓃᑦ ᑐᓕᒫᕕᓂᖏᓐᓂᒃ ᐱᖄᑲᖅᐸᓚᐅᓇᓪᓗᑎᒃ ᐱᐊᒃᓴᖅᓯᒪᓪᓗᒍ. ᖃᒧᔨᐊᖑᔪᑦ ᐊᑦᑕᕐᓇᐃᔭᖅᓯᒪᕙᒃᐳᑦ ᐅᕿᓐᓇᓱᐊᖅᓲᑎᒡᓗ ᐅᓯᔪᓐᓇᕐᑯᓪᓗᑎᑦ ᐱᕐᑯᑎᓕᒫᖏᓐᓂᒃ ᐃᓄᖕᓂᒡᓗ ᐅᖓᓯᒃᑐᒧᑦ ᓯᑯᒃᑯᑦ ᓄᓇᒃᑯᓪᓗ. ᕿᒧᒃᓯᐅᑕᐅᕙᓚᐅᖅᐳᑦ ᐃᑏᓐᓂᓗ ᐃᓄᐃᓐᓇᕐᓄᑦ ᐅᓂᐊᖅᑕᐅᕙᒃᓱᑎᒃ. ᐋᖅᑭᐅᒪᑦᑎᐊᖅᑎᑕᐅᓇᓱᒃᐸᓚᐅᖅᐳᑦ ᖃᐅᑕᒫᑦᑎᐊᖅ ᐊᑐᕐᓇᑦᑎᐊᕐᑯᓪᓗᑎᑦ ᐊᖅᑯᓪᓘᑕᐅᓕᓗᐊᒃᑯᑦ.

ᐅᓪᓗᒥ ᓱᓕ ᓴᓇᒪᓂᖅᑲᑦᑎᐊᓇᐊᖅᑲᖅᐳᑦ ᖃᐅᔨᒪᑦᑎᐊᓇᐊᖅᑲᕐᓗᒍᓗ ᐋᖅᑭᑦᓯᒪᓂᖓ ᐊᓯᔾᔨᖅᓯᒪᓗᐊᖃᓂᓗ ᓴᓇᔾᔪᓯᐅᕙᒃᑐᑐᖅᑲᕐᒥᑦ. ᓄᓇᖅᑲᑎᒌᖕᒋᑦᑐᑦ ᐊᔾᔨᒌᖖᒋᐊᕐᔪᒃᑐᒥᒃ ᖃᒧᔨᐅᕈᓯᖅᑲᖅᐸᒃᐳᑦ ᐊᑐᕈᑎᒃᓴᖕᒐᓄᑦᓗ ᐋᖅᑭᑦᑕᐅᓯᒪᓇᓱᐊᖅᑐᓂ. ᓴᓇᔭᐅᓯᒪᓇᓱᐊᖅᐸᒃᐳᑦ ᕿᕋᑕᓗᐊᖅᑎᑦᑕᐃᓕᑦᓗᒍ, ᐋᖅᑭᐅᒪᑦᑎᐊᕈᓐᓇᕐᑯᓪᓗᒍ ᒪᓃᓚᖅᓯᐅᕈᑕᐅᔪᓐᓇᕐᓗᓂ. ᓇᐳᑦᑕᖅᓱᖅᑕᐅᓲᖑᔪᑦ ᐊᒃᓱᓈᒧᑦ ᑭᑭᐊᒃᑐᓚᐅᓇᑎᒃ ᕿᕋᑕᓗᐊᖅᑯᓇᒍ ᐊᑦᑕᕐᓇᓗᐊᖅᑯᓇᒍᓗ ᒪᓃᓛᖅᓯᐅᕈᑕᐅᕙᖕᒪᑕ ᐅᑭᐅᖅᑕᖅᑐᒥ. ᑖᓐᓇ ᓴᓇᔭᐅᒪᓂᖓ ᐊᑐᖅᑕᐅᓯᒪᕗᖅ ᕿᑭᑦᑖᓗᑉ ᐅᐊᖕᓇᖓᓂᕐᒥᐅᓄᑦ.

BACKGROUND

Early qamutiik frames were made from whalebone, driftwood, antlers, and sealskin rope. The runners were made from frozen fish held together with frozen caribou or walrus skin. The running surface was prepared from either moistened moss, covered in layers of ice, or the rib of a bowhead whale, covered in ice. It was an art to build a sturdy but light qamutiik in order to haul belongings and people over huge distances of ice and snow. These sleds were hauled by dogs and sometimes by people. Maintenance of these sleds was done every day to keep them performing well in the harshest of conditions.

Today's qamutiit still require a lot of skill to build and are based on the same principles as earlier sleds. There are many different variations of qamutiit, depending on the region of the North in which they are being used. The principle of the qamutiit is for it not to be rigid, but to be able to flex and move with the surface of the ice. Tying the qamutiik with rope rather than nails or screws allows for this flexibility and durability, which is essential in the harsh and rough conditions of the Arctic. This account describes the steps used in the construction of a North Baffin qamutiik.

ᖃᒧᑏᒃ QAMUTIIK

ᐅᑦᓱᒃᓴᐃᓂᖅ
SHAPE RUNNERS

ᐋᖅᑭᒃᓯᒪᓂᓇᒐᔭᖅᑕᖕᒥᑦ ᑭᑦᓗᕐᓗᒥᑦ. ᐅᐃᕐᓂᖓ ᐃᖅᑯᐊᓗ ᐋᖅᑭᒃᑕᐅᓯᒪᓲᖑᔪᑦ ᐊᑐᖅᑕᐅᖃᑦᑕᕐᓂᓇᒐᔭᖅᑕᖕᒐᓄᑦ.

Rough out the shape of the runners with a skill saw or jigsaw. The shape of the front and rear is dependent on ice and snow conditions.

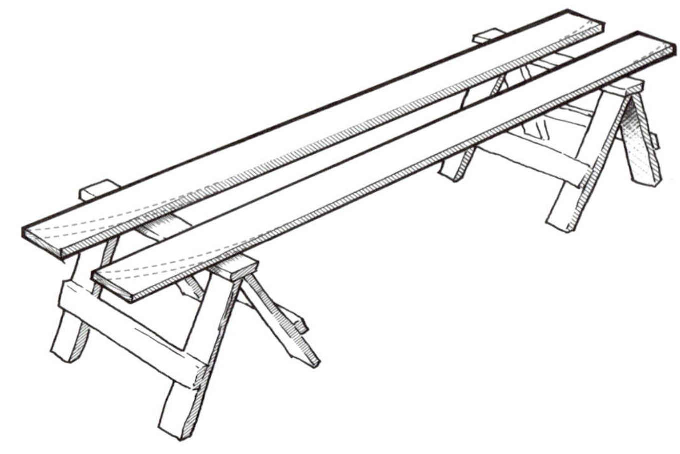

ᐸᑎᒃᑎᑦᓗᒋᒃ
JOIN RUNNERS

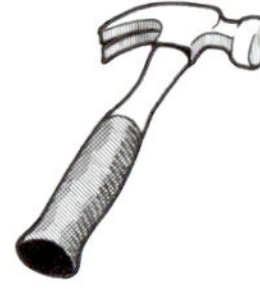

ᑭᑭᐊᒡᔪᐊᕐᒧᑦ ᐸᑎᒃᑎᓯᒪᑲᐃᓐᓇᕈᓐᓇᖅᑐᑦ.

Temporarily join the runners together with spikes.

ᐅᕙ�XXX

ᖃᒧᑏᒃ QAMUTIIK

ᐅᐃᕐᓂᖅᑭᒃ ᕿᖅᓱᑕᓇᐊᖅᑲᕐᓂᖅᑭᑦ
REINFORCE FRONT

ᐊᒥᖅᑕᒧᑦ ᕿᕋᑕᓗᐊᖅᑭᑦᑐᒧᑦ ᕿᖅᓱᑕᕐᓗᒍ ᑭᑭᐊᒃᑐᕈᓐᓇᕐᓗᒍ ᑭᑭᐊᑐᐃᓐᓇᕐᓄᑦ ᕿᔾᔮᓚᖕᓄᑦ ᓅᓐᓃᑦ ᐊᑦᑐᖅᑭᕈᓐᓇᖅᑐᖅ.

Use light- or medium-gauge sheet metal to reinforce the front section of the runners. Attach with screws or ribbed nails.

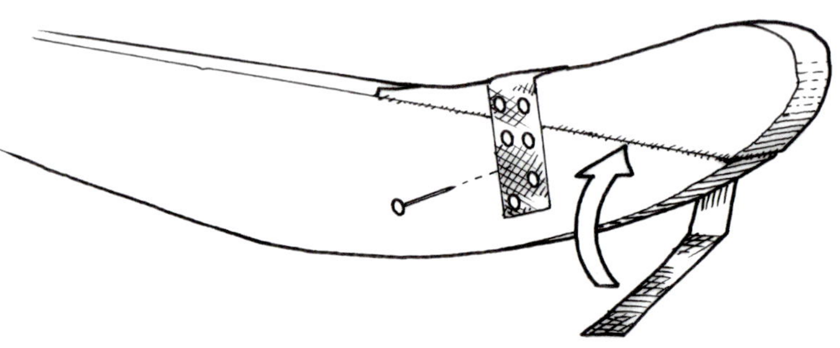

ᓇᐳᓚᐅᓯᕐᕕᒃᓴᖅᑭᑦ
DRILL HOLES

ᓇᐳᓚᐅᓯᕐᕕᓚᐅᕈᓐᓇᖅᑐᖅ ᐊᔾᔨᙱᒍᐊᖅ ᒪᓚᒡᓗᒍ. ᓇᓚᒧᑏᑭᐊᖅᑲᖅᑭᑦᑐᑦ ᖁᐱᓴᕋᐃᖁᓇᒍ. ᐊᔪᑎᕐᔫᒥᓗᑭᓪᓗ ᓇᐳᓚᐅᑎᖕᑭᓐᓂᒃ ᓄᖑᕋᐃᖁᓇᒍ.

Drill holes in the runners as pictured below. Make sure the holes are offset to reduce the possibility of cracking. Round off the holes to minimize rope fraying.

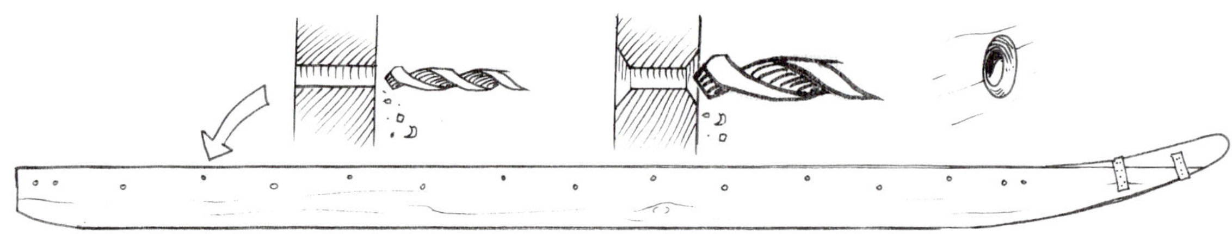

ᓇᐳᓚᐅᕐᓂᖅ
CUT NAPUIT

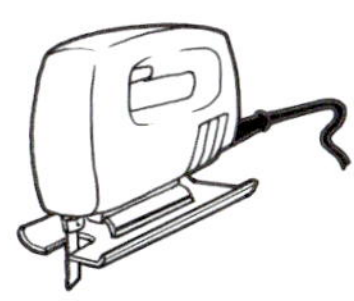

ᓇᐳᓚᐅᓯᕐᕕᒃᓴᓚᐅᕐᓗᒋᑦ. ᐊᔾᔨᒌᙱᑦᑐᓂᒃ ᓇᐳᓚᐅᕈᓯᕐᑲᐅᕈᓐᓇᖅᑐᑦ. ᑎᓴᒃᑕᐃᑦ ᐊᑦᑕᕐᓇᙱᓐᓂᖅᓴᐅᔪᓐᓇᖅᐳᑦ ᐊᑐᕐᑲᐅᔾᔪᓐᓇᕐᓂᖅᓴᐅᓪᓗᑎᒡᓗ.

Cut crossmembers (*napuit*). There is wide variation in the shape and style of napuit. Generally hardwoods will last longer.

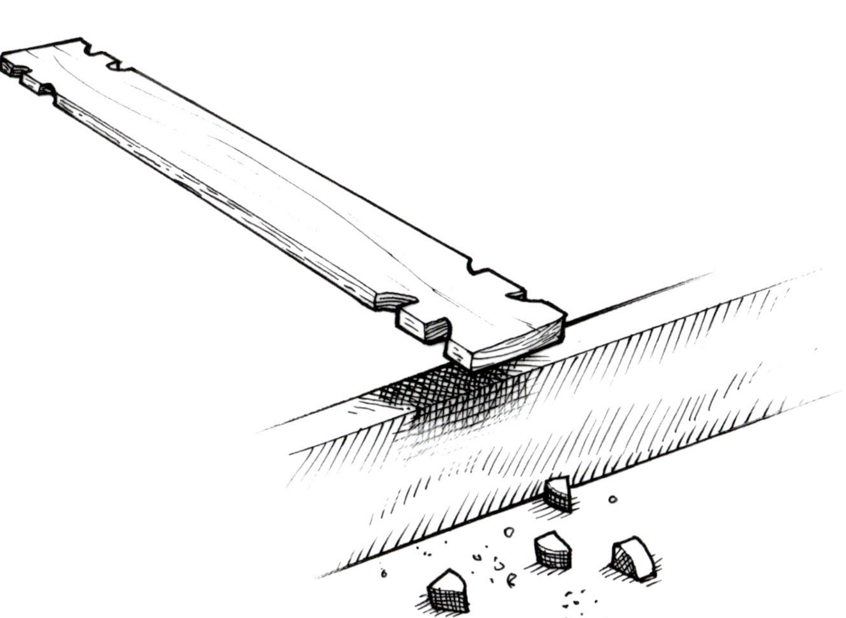

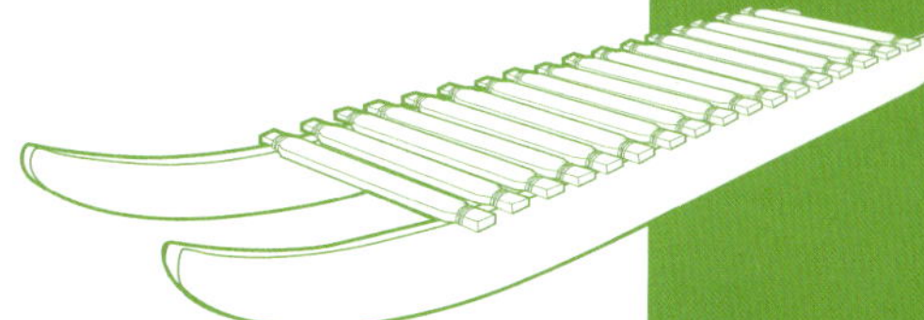

ᖃᒧᑏᒃ QAMUTIIK

ᓇᐳᕐᕆᑦ ᓯᕗᓪᓚᖅᐹᖅ ᑭᖑᓪᓚᖅᐹᕐᓗ
FIRST/LAST NAPU
(ᓯᕗᓂᐊᓂ ᐃᖅᑯᐊᓂᓗ/FRONT TO BACK)

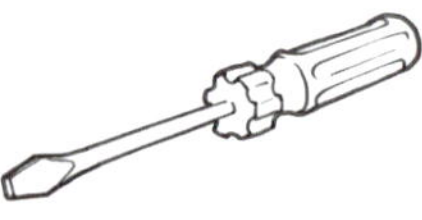

1 ᓇᐳᓕᐅᑏᑦ ᐳᑐᕐᕿᑎᒍᑦ ᓄᕕᐅᕋᕐᓗᒍ ᓇᓗᓇᐃᖅᓯᒪᔪᑦ ᒪᓕᒡᓗᒍ.

Feed the rope through the holes in the runners as indicated.

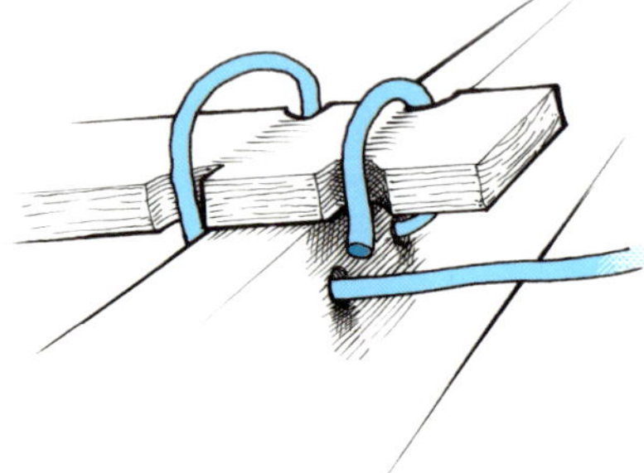

2 ᒪᕐᕈᐃᖅᓱᒃᑲᓐᓂᕐᓗᒍ ᓯᕗᓪᓕᐅᖅᑲᐅᔪᑎᑐᑦ. ᓱᒃᑕᐃᓕᑲᓚᐅᕐᓗᒍ. ᐃᓱᐊᒍᑦ ᐳᑐᓕᐅᕐᓗᒍ.

Feed the rope twice more, as in step one. Do not tighten. Create a loop at the end of the rope.

3 ᓄᕕᓗᒍ ᐳᑐᓕᐊᕆᕋᑖᖅᑕᒃᑯᑦ.

Feed the loose end of the rope through the loop you created.

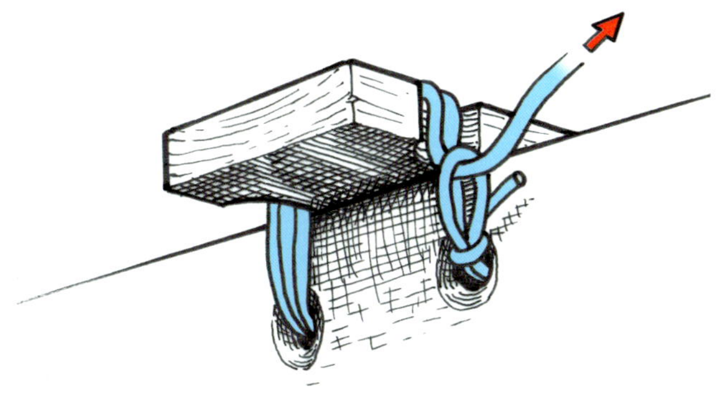

4 ᓱᑲᑎᖅᐸᓪᓚᐊᓗᒍ ᕿᓚᕈᑎᖃᕐᓂᖓᓂᑦ ᐱᒋᐊᕐᓗᒍ.

Tighten the rope so that the loop is just protruding from the hole in the runner.

5 ᒪᓕᒃᐸᓪᓚᐊᓗᒋᑦ ᖃᓱᖕᒐᓂᖕᒋᑦ. ᐊᑐᓂ ᓱᑲᑎᖅᐸᓪᓚᐊᔪᓇᐊᖅᑕᖅᑐᑦ.

Tighten the free end of the rope. You may have to tighten each round of rope separately.

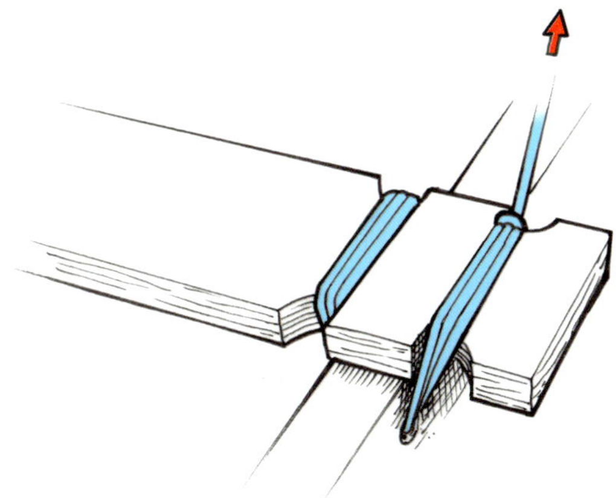

6 ᕿᔾᔮᖅᓯᓯᒧᑦ ᐊᔪᓪᓗᒍ. ᐃᓱᐊ ᓄᖁᐅᖅᑲᕐᓗᒍ ᐊᑦᑐᖕᒋᐅᑎᒋᓗᒍ ᕿᓚᒡᓗᒍᓗ

Lift the outside round of rope slightly with a screwdriver. Feed the loose end of the rope under and repeat many times.
Tie off with a half-hitch knot.

ᓇᐳᓕᖅᓯᐃᓂᖅ
TYING NAPU
(ᓯᕗᓂᐊᓂ ᐃᖅᑯᐊᓂᓗ/FRONT TO BACK)

1 ᐃᓗᖕᒫᖕᒪᓂᑦ ᓄᕕᓗᒍ.

Insert a loop into a hole from the inside of the runner.

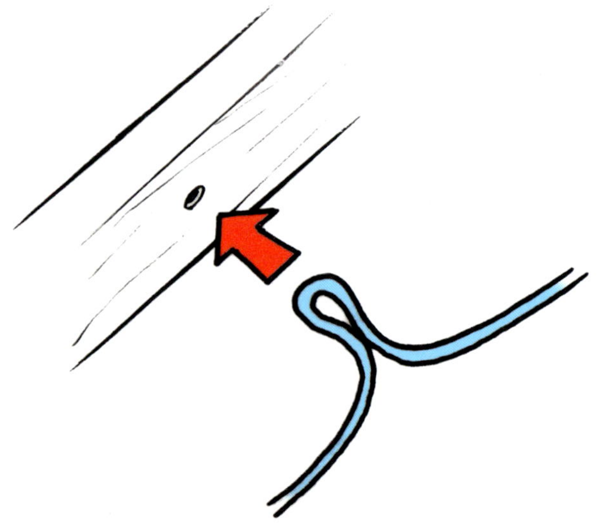

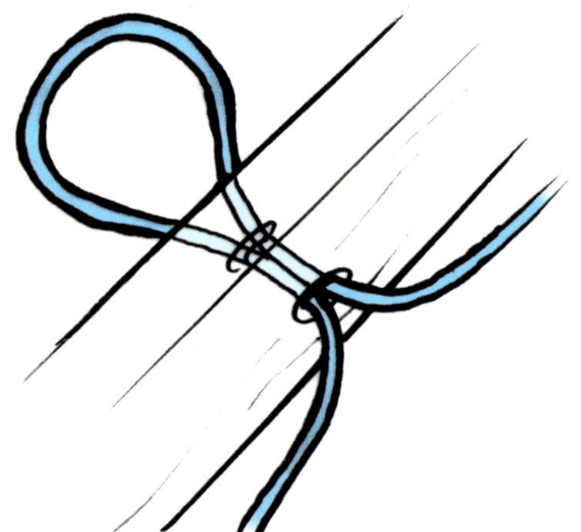

2 ᓯᓚᑖᓃᓐᓂᖅᓴᖅ ᓂᑭᑦᑐᓇᐊᕐᓗᒍ.

Enlarge the loop on the outside of the runner.

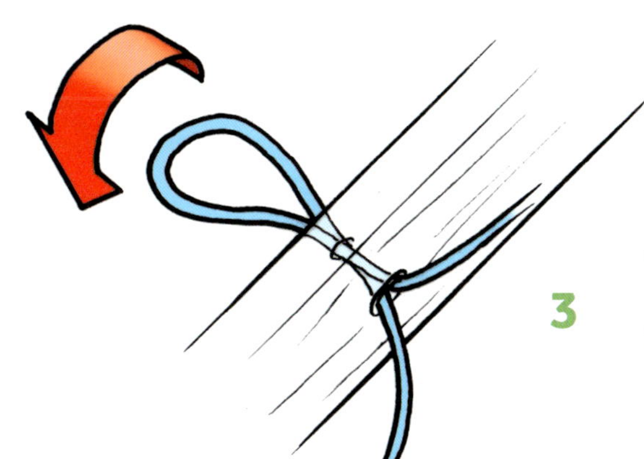

3

ᐊᑕᐅᓯᐊᕐᓗᒍ ᑭᔅᔭᕐᓗᖅᑎᓪᓗᒍ.

Twist the loop once.

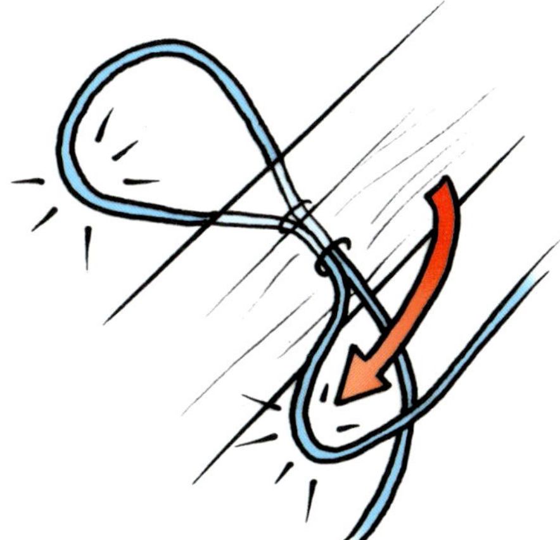

4

ᐳᑐᖅᑲᓕᖅᑎᓪᓗᒍ ᐃᓗᖔᖓ ᓇᓗᓇᐃᖅᓯᒪᓂᖓ
ᒪᓕᒃᓗᒍ. ᑎᒍᓗᒍ ᐳᑐᓕᐅᖅᓯᒪᕙᖅ

Create a loop on the inside of the runner as indicated. Grab the loops as indicated.

5

ᕿᔅᔭᕐᓗᕐᓗᒍ ᐊᑕᐅᓯᐊᕐᓗᒍ.

Twist once, as indicated.

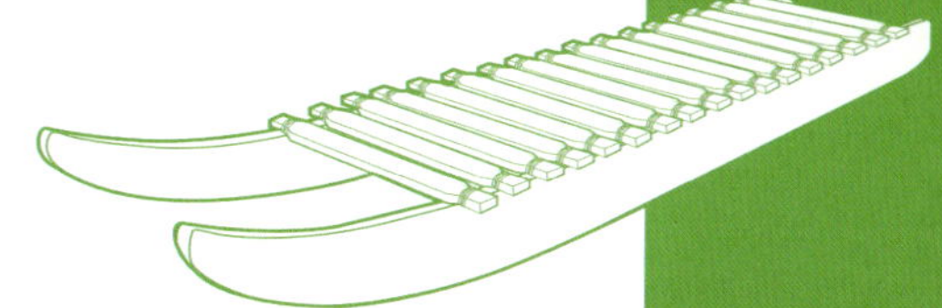

ᖃᒧᑏᒃ QAMUTIIK

6 ᕐᑯᒻᒧᒃᑎᓪᓗᒍ ᓇᐳᐊ ᐃᓗᖅᑯᖅᑐᓈᕐᑯᓪᓗᒍ.

Lift the loops in preparation for the *napu*.

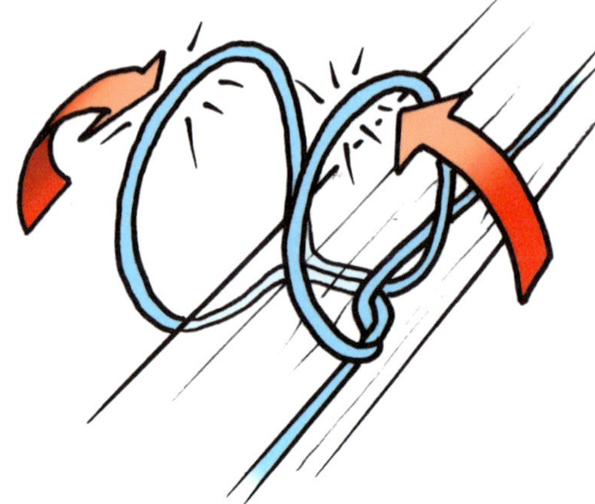

7 ᓇᐳᓕᐊᓪᓚᓚᐅᕐᓗᒍ ᓯᓚᑎᖕᒫᖕᒪᓂᑦ ᓱᑲᖅᑳᕐᓗᒍ.

Insert the napu. Tighten the outside loop first.

8 ᐃᓚᖕᒐ ᓱᑲᓕᕐᒥᓗᒍ ᓇᐳᐊ ᐊᐅᓚᑎᓪᓗᒍ ᓱᑲᑦᑎᐊᕈᓐᓇᕐᑯᓪᓗᒍ. ᓇᐳᓕᐊᑖ ᓱᑲᑦᑎᐊᕈᓂ ᐃᒻᒥᓂᒃ ᐊᑦᑐᖕᒋᐅᑎᒋᔪᖅ

Tighten remaining rope and move the napu back and forth while pulling the rope, so the napu seats itself tightly. Once tight, this knot is self-locking.

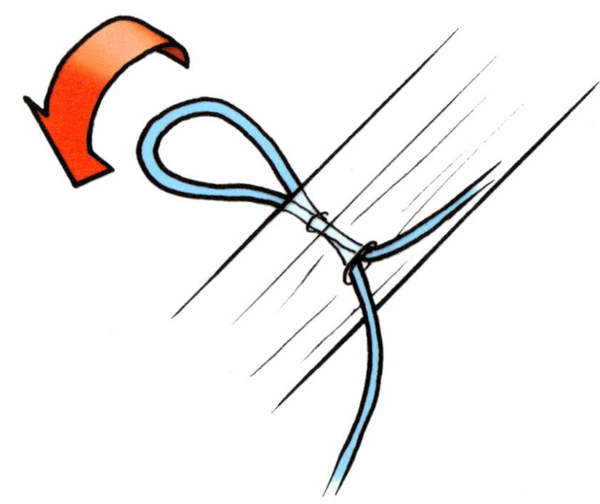

ᐱᕐᖀᖅᑭᑦ
SLIDERS

1 ᐱᕐᖀᒃᓴᖅᑭᑦ ᕿᔾᔮᓚᖅᒧᑦ ᑭᑭᐊᒃᑐᕐᓗᑭᑦ. ᐃᓗᕙᓯᑭᐊᖃᖅᑐᑦ ᐱᕐᕿᔾᔦᖅᓲᑎᑭᔾᑎᑦ.

Screw nylon “sliders” to the bottom of the runners as indicated. Make sure that the screws are countersunk.

2 ᐊᒥᖅᑕᒧᑦ ᐃᔾᔪᓗᐊᖅᑭᑦᑐᒧᑦ ᓯᕗᓂᐊ ᖃᓚᐊᕈᓯᕐᓗᒍ. ᐊᖅᑭᓂᖅᓴᐅᕌᕐᔪᒍᓐᓇᖅᑐᖅ ᖃᓚᐊᕈᓯᐅᑎᔭᐃᑦ.

Use medium-gauge sheet metal to reinforce the “noses” of the runners. Leave at least a three-quarter-inch overhang on the sides.

3 ᒪᖑᒃᑎᐅᖅᑲᕐᓗᒍ ᑕᒪᓐᓇ ᑭᒡᓚᖓ.

Hammer down the overhanging sheet metal to protect the edges of the wood.

ᖃᐅᔨᒪᔭᕆᐊᓖᑦ ᐱᔪᓐᓇᕈᑕᐅᕙᒃᑐᑦᓗ
TIPS AND TRICKS

ᐅᐃᖅᓂᖓ:
ᐅᐃᖅᓂᖓᑕ ᖃᐅᖓ ᐊᔾᔨᒌᖑᓐᓇᖅᑦᑕᖏᑦᑐᖅ ᓯᓇᒧᑦ ᐊᑐᖅᑐᒃᓴᐅᓂᐊ ᒪᓚᒃᓗᒍ- ᒪᓂᓚᖅᓯᐅᕈᑕᐅᕙᒃᑐᑦ ᐅᐃᖅᓂᖅᑯᖅᑐᓂᖅᓴᐅᕙᒃᐳᑦ ᒪᓂᕿᐃᓐᓇᒃᑰᕈᑕᐅᕙᒃᑐᑦ ᐅᐃᖅᓂᑯᑖᖅᑲᖅᓂᖅᓴᐅᕙᒃᐳᑦ.

ᐊᑐᖁᔭᖅᑐᑦ ᖃᒧᑎᒃᓴᐅᓗᑎᒃ:
ᖃᒧᑎᒃᓴᓂᒐᓱᖕᓂᐊᕐᓗᓂ ᐅᔾᔨᕆᔭᕆᐊᖅᑲᖅᑐᑦ ᖁᑉᐸᖅᑲᓗᐊᖏᓪᓗᓂ ᐊᑭᕈᖅᑲᓗᐊᖏᓪᓗᓂᓗ

ᓇᐳᓕᐅᑎᒃᓴᖅ ᐊᒃᓗᓈᖅ:
ᓇᐳᓕᐅᑎᒋᓂᐊᖅᑕᐃᑦ ᓯᓚᓗᐊᕆᐊᖅᑲᖏᒻᒥᔭᖅ ᐃᒻᒪᖄ ᐃᖅᑭᖅᑯᖅᓂᑦ ᑐᐊᓐᓂᖅᓴᐅᖄᖅᔭᓪᓗᒍ ᖃᓯᔭᓗᐊᕆᐊᖅᑲᓂᓗ. ᑲᓗᑎᒃᓴᐃᑦ ᑎᑭᖅᑐᑦ ᓯᓚᒃᑎᒋᔭᕆᐊᖅᑲᖅᑐᖅ ᑕᑭᔪᐊᓘᖏᑦᑐᓂᓗ ᖃᒧᑎᖓᓂᑦ ᑕᑭᓂᖅᓴᐅᑲᑦᓚᒡᓗᒍ.

ᐱᖅᓰᖏᑦ:
ᓯᕗᓂᐊᒍᑦ ᐃᓚᙵᓇᐊᖅᑲᖅᑐᖅ ᐊᑦᑕᖅᓇᖏᓐᓂᖅᓴᐅᔭᓐᓇᖅᑯᑦᓗᒍ ᐅᓯᖅᔭᐊᖅᑲᑦᑕᖅᓂᐊᖅᓗᓂ ᐅᖅᑯᒪᐃᑦᑐᓂᒃ. ᐱᖅᓰᖓ ᖃᒧᑎᒃᓴᒥᑦ ᓯᓚᖕᓂᖅᓴᐅᔭᕆᐊᖅᒥᔪᑦ ᓱᖕᒍᖅᐃᓗᐊᖅᑯᓇᒍ ᖃᒧᑎᑕᖕᒐᓂᒃ.

Nose:
The curvature of the nose of the qamutiik depends on the terrain it will be used in—rough, jumbled ice requires a more curved nose, while smooth, flat ice requires a more gently sloping nose.

Wood Material:
If choosing solid wood for the runners, make sure there are no cracks or serious knots. Plywood can be used to face the runners for added strength. Hardwoods such as walnut or oak are ideal for napuit.

Rope:
For tying the napuit, use rope no thicker than a quarter of an inch, which doesn't slip on itself when tied in a knot. For a pulling rope, choose a material that doesn't stretch too much, and is at least half an inch and at least one-and-a-half times as long as the qamutiik.

Runners:
Plane the runners to about an eight-degree slope—this provides stability and strength when carrying a load. Nylon sliders should be slightly wider than the runners to prevent damage to the wood.

© RON WASSINK

ᑎᑎᕋᖅᑑᑉ ᒥᒃᓵᓄᑦ

ᓲᓗᒨᓂ ᐊᕙ ᐃᓅᓯᒪᔪᖅ ᖃᕐᒪᒥ, ᐃᒡᓗᓕᐅᑉ ᖃᓂᒋᔮᖓᓂ ᑐᓴᖅᑑᑦ/ᓅᕙᐃᕝᕙ 2, 1959ᒥ. ᒥᑭᔫᓂᕐᒥᓂᒃ ᑭᓯᓕᒫᓂᒃ ᐊᕙᑎᒥᓂᒃ ᑐᑭᓯᔪᒪᖃᑦᑕᓚᐅᖅᑐᖅ. ᒥᖅᓱᕆᐅᓚᐅᖅᑐᖅ ᕿᓯᓐᓂᒃ ᐊᓈᓇᒥᓂᒃ ᐃᓕᑦᓯᓂ, ᐊᐱᐊ ᐊᕙᒥᒃ. ᐊᑖᑕᒋᓚᐅᖅᑕᖓ ᒪᑕᐃᐊᓯ ᐊᕙ, ᓴᓇᙳᐊᖅᓯᑕᐅᓚᐅᖅᑐᖅ, ᐱᓗᐊᖅᑐᒥ ᑑᒐᕐᓂᒃ- ᐃᓚᖓᓐᓂ ᐅᓈᓕᐅᖅᑐᒥᓂᖅ ᑐᒃᑑᑉ ᓇᒡᔪᖏᓐᓂᒃ ᐅᓐᓄᐃᓐᓇᖅ--ᓲᓗᒨᓂᐅᑉ ᐃᓕᕝᕕᒋᓯᒪᔪᖓ ᓴᓇᙳᐊᕐᓂᕐᒥᒃ.

ᓲᓗᒨᓂ ᐃᖖᒋᕆᐅᓚᐅᖅᑐᖅ ᒥᑭᔫᑦᓯᓂ ᐃᓚᒋᔭᐅᑦᓯᓂ ᐅᑦᑐᒥᓂᓴᕐᓄᑦ ᓂᔾᔭᐅᓯᔭᖅᑎᓄᑦ. ᐊᔾᔨᒌᙱᑦᑐᓂᒃ ᓂᔾᔭᐅᓯᔭᕆᑎᓂᒃ ᐱᙳᐊᕆᓐᓇᖅᑐᖅ, ᓲᕐᓗ ᐱᐊᓇᒥᒃ. ᑎᑎᕋᕆᓐᓇᖅᓯᓂᓗ ᐃᖖᒋᒐᕐᓂᒃ ᐃᓄᒃᑎᑐᑦ. ᓴᓇᖃᑦᑕᕐᒥᔪᖅ ᕿᓚᐅᑎᓂᒃ ᐸᐃᓇᕕᓐᓄᑦ, ᐃᓕᓐᓂᐊᕐᕕᓐᓄᑦ ᑭᒃᑯᐃᓐᓇᕐᓄᓪᓗ ᐱᑖᕈᒪᔪᓄᑦ.

ᖁᕕᐊᒋᔭᖃᕐᒥᔪᖅ ᐅᓂᒃᑳᓕᐊᖅ ᐃᓕᓚᐅᖅᑕᒥᓂᒃ ᐊᑖᑕᒥᓂᒃ. ᐅᓂᒃᑳᖃᑦᑕᖅᑐᖅ ᐃᓕᓐᓂᐊᕐᕕᓐᓂ, ᓄᕝᕗᖅᑭᐅᓪᓚᐃᓪᓗ ᓄᓇᖓᓐᓅᕈᓐᓇᓚᐅᕐᒥᔪᖅ ᐅᓂᒃᑳᓕᐊᖅᑐᖅᓯᓐᓈᑦ ᑕᒪᒃᑯᓂᖓ. ᐃᓕᓐᓂᐊᑎᑦᓯᖃᑦᑕᖅᑐᖅ ᐃᓄᐃᑦ ᐃᓕᖅᑯᓯᖏᓐᓂᒃ ᓄᓇᕗᒻᒥ ᓯᓚᑦᑐᓴᕐᕕᒻᒥ. ᐃᖅᑲᓇᐃᔭᖅᑐᖅ ᐃᓄᐃᑦ ᐅᖃᐅᓯᖏᓐᓂᒃ ᑕᐃᒎᓯᓕᐅᖅᑎᒃᑯᓐᓄᑦ.

ABOUT THE AUTHOR

Solomon Awa was born in a sod house near Iglulik on November 2, 1959. From a young age, he was curious about everything around him. He learned to sew traditional items such as sealskins from his late mother, Appia Awa. His late father, Mathias Awa, was an excellent carver, especially with ivory—one time he made a harpoon from caribou antlers in one night—and Solomon learned to carve from him.

Solomon started singing at a young age in a contemporary band. He plays many instruments, including organ, and writes songs in Inuktitut. He also handcrafts drums for daycares, local schools, and various other places.

He loves to tell the stories that he learned from his father. He does this at schools, and also had the opportunity to go to Kaotokeno, Norway, to tell some of these stories. He teaches traditional knowledge at Nunavut Arctic College and works for the Inuit Uqausinginnik Taiguusiliuqtit.

Iqaluit • Toronto